Do Haunted Houses Exist?

Other titles in the *Do They Exist?* series include:

Do Aliens Exist?

Do Dragons Exist?

Do Ghosts Exist?

Do Vampires Exist?

Do Witches Exist?

Do Haunted Houses Exist?

Jenny MacKay

ReferencePoint
Press®

San Diego, CA

LIBRARY OF CONGRESS CATALOGING-IN-PUBLICATION DATA

MacKay, Jenny, 1978- author.
  Do haunted houses exist? / by Jenny MacKay.
    pages cm. -- (Do they exist?)
  Audience: Grades 9 to 12.
  Includes bibliographical references and index.
  ISBN-13: 978-1-60152-858-2 (hardback)
  ISBN-10: 1-60152-858-2 (hardback) 1. Haunted houses--Juvenile literature. 2. Ghosts--Juvenile literature. I. Title.
  BF1475.M25 2016
  133.1'22--dc23
                                                              2015017840

Contents

What Are Haunted Houses?

Merriam-Webster's Collegiate Dictionary provides multiple meanings for the word *haunt*, including "to visit often," "to have a disquieting or harmful effect on," "to recur constantly and spontaneously," "to linger," and "to visit or inhabit as a ghost." The same dictionary defines the word *ghost* as "a disembodied soul," especially "the soul of a dead person believed to be an inhabitant of the unseen world or to appear to the living in bodily likeness."[1] Haunted houses, then, can be defined as places that have—or are said to have—unsettling effects from a presence that lingers, recurs, or spontaneously appears.

Many people do not believe in inhabitants of an unseen world. Even among those who do there is no absolute agreement about the factors that would define such an inhabitant or what clues it might reveal to indicate its presence. People in one house might hear footsteps, knocking, or voices in empty rooms. Those in another might see shadows, balls of light, moving objects, or images that seem to be people until they disappear or walk through walls or closed doors. Sudden drops in temperature, the feeling of a breeze brushing across one's skin, and even the sensation of being hit or scratched have been described in haunted buildings. Strange smells such as a particular perfume or an unexplained metallic taste are considered other possibly sensory experiences that believers think could indicate a haunting.

Some believers in haunted houses link almost anything out of the ordinary—even something such as feeling dizzy or nauseated—to potential evidence of ghostly activity, but there is no checklist of phenomena that occur in all haunted buildings. Some people claim to see images of people who resemble former residents of the building but who disappear when someone tries to talk to them. Others claim to have seen apparitions that try to interact with them by talking, moving objects, or even touching them. Still other people say they are tormented by poltergeists (German for "knocking spirit"), unseen but mischievous or even dangerous presences that make loud noises, move or throw objects, and can even hit, shove, or otherwise harass living people. Any of the above experiences and many more could all be considered signs of a haunting by people who believe. The lack of a formal and recurring list of experiences common to all haunted houses is one of the things that leads to skepticism about whether they really exist.

The Image of a Haunted House

Although haunted houses lack any formally descriptive definition, most people readily recognize features of a home that looks as though it could be haunted. Young children in the United States are exposed to images of haunted houses in picture books, in cartoons like *Scooby-Doo*, on bags of Halloween candy, and even at a Disneyland attraction called the Haunted Mansion. In this way, society may condition people, especially children, to link certain factors such as the sight of neglected older buildings or the sound of squeaking shutters or whistling wind with fear or dread. "The allure of this stereotypical haunted house is universal and easily understood,"[2] say historians Gary D. Joiner and Cheryl H. White.

> "The allure of this stereotypical haunted house is universal and easily understood."[2]
>
> —Historians Gary D. Joiner and Cheryl H. White.

Universal familiarity with the concept of a haunted house only seems to have fed a longstanding disagreement about whether such places are truly infested with restless spirits or whether ghostly phenomena are merely a figment of the imagination. The subject has long been a source of debate between skeptics and believers. About 40 percent of Americans believe that certain buildings

A worn and rickety-looking house, surrounded by a neglected yard, has "haunted" written all over it. Although there is no agreed-upon definition of a haunted house, characteristics like these strongly suggest a building where restless spirits reside.

contain and are haunted by the spiritual remains of people whose physical bodies have died. The rest of the population turns a doubtful eye toward the idea of hauntings, believing they are little more than evidence of superstitious minds and overly active imaginations. The popularity of books, movies, and television documentaries featuring haunted spaces only seems to make believers more adamant in their acceptance of these phenomena while turning skeptics even more staunchly against what they think are theatrics.

Real Haunted Estates

Despite differing views about the reality of haunted houses, American law actually validates the possibility that they may exist. The real estate industry, which deals with the buying and selling of houses and property, is tasked with setting fair policies for the transfer of land and buildings from one owner to another. For example, sellers who know a home is infested with mold or has a structural problem cannot hide this information. In many states, real estate law goes a step further by including a negative reputation or stigma, such as rumors of paranormal phenomena, among things a seller must disclose to a buyer who asks.

According to *Rhode Island Real Estate Basics*, "A stigmatized or psychologically impacted property is one that has acquired an undesirable reputation for a problem that is unrelated to a physical defect. . . . Stigmatized properties include those properties where a murder, suicide, or felony occurred or is suspected to have occurred."[3] Often such a home gains a reputation as being haunted, which can make it difficult to sell. Sometimes homeowners who believe their home is haunted are so eager to move out that they offer their home at a very low selling price. This itself is often considered a red flag to buyers—a warning that a home harbors unsettling characteristics beneath what often seems to be a perfectly charming exterior. The need for laws that address such stigmas suggests the belief in haunted houses is alive in modern American society, as it has been worldwide for centuries.

Chapter 1

Why Do People Believe in Haunted Houses?

"What we have is people trying to make sense of something that, to them, seems inexplicable. So you get the misinterpretation of noises or visual effects that do have a normal explanation, but not one that people can think of. People assume that if they cannot explain something in natural terms, then it must be something paranormal."

—Christopher French, psychology professor and head of the Anomalistic Psychology Research Unit at Goldsmiths, University of London.

Quoted in Tiffanie Wen, "Why Do People Believe in Ghosts?," *The Atlantic*, September 5, 2014. www.theatlantic.com.

"Brilliant scientists believe in lots of things for which there is no evidence, like multiverses and superstrings and God. . . . I think if psi [paranormal phenomena] was real, someone would surely have provided irrefutable proof of it by now. But how I wish that someone would find such proof!"

—Science journalist and technology instructor John Horgan.

John Horgan, "Brilliant Scientists Are Open-Minded About Paranormal Stuff, So Why Not You?," *Scientific American*, July 20, 2012. http://blogs.scientificamerican.com.

The notion that human structures can be haunted by spirits or mysterious presences is ancient and also nearly universal among human cultures. Beliefs about haunted places exist worldwide, and some stories and descriptions are thousands of years old. No matter when or where tales of hauntings occur, they generally describe very similar phenomena that have been unnerving people since the dawn of human history. "Ghosts and spirits are as old as mankind," says anthropologist and paranormal investigator Robert James Wlodarski. "Ghosts remain a part of every culture, a testament to the fact that we cannot control everything, or know everything, and some things must be taken on faith or left to a higher source to ultimately explain."[4] For many people, the universal human belief in haunted structures is convincing evidence that they exist.

Hauntings Since the Dawn of History

The earliest known accounts of ghosts and hauntings come from the ancient culture of Mesopotamia. Located in a region called the Fertile Crescent between the Tigris and Euphrates Rivers of the Middle East, Mesopotamia is believed to have been the first human civilization, originating in about 3500 BCE. According to written records they left behind, Mesopotamians believed that the living and the dead inhabited separate realms or worlds. Once a person died, his or her soul left its physical body and went to another realm. However, they also believed souls could return—especially if the person had died in an unnatural or violent way or if the physical body had not been given what the Mesopotamians believed was a proper funeral and burial.

> "Ghosts remain a part of every culture, a testament to the fact that we cannot control everything, or know everything."[4]
>
> —Anthropologist and paranormal investigator Robert James Wlodarski.

For Mesopotamians, the spirit of a dead person who returned to bother the living was unnatural, frightening, and a sign of evil. A Mesopotamian story called *Gilgamesh*, written on stone tablets in about 2000 BCE, is the oldest existing written story ever discovered. Parts of it mention ghosts of people who died in unnatural ways or whose spirits cannot rest. One line of the story describes a man who was cursed by his parents before death: "He was deprived of an heir; his ghost still roams." Another line tells what became of a man whose body was never properly buried: "His

The ancient Egyptians believed that spirits roamed the massive pyramids at Giza. These spirits served as guardians of the pharaohs and the treasures that were entombed with them.

ghost is not at rest in the Netherworld."[5] Although regarded today as a fictional tale, *Gilgamesh* shows that the idea of restless ghosts haunting the world of the living has existed for millennia.

Ancient Egyptians also told stories of spirits and haunted places. Like the Mesopotamians, Egyptians believed in an afterlife, and they developed complex rituals for preparing a deceased person's body so that his or her soul could enter the other realm. Because Egyptians believed the other realm to be more pleasant than the living world, they thought any spirits that returned were evil or were being punished for wicked deeds. Ghosts of different sorts were rumored to roam in the Giza pyramids, the tombs of the pharaohs that were built between about 2575 and 2150 BCE. These ghosts supposedly served as guardians of the royal inhabitants and their treasures. "The pyramids were said to be haunted by living spirits who would keep out all intruders other than those worthy of admission,"[6] say Egyptologists Robert M. Schoch and

Robert Aquinas McNally. Tales of the supernatural have always surrounded the pyramids and are among the earliest and most enduring human accounts of haunted structures.

Ghosts of Ancient Greece and Rome

Ancient Greeks and Romans also told stories of ghosts and hauntings. People of both cultures believed that spirits moved to another realm after bodily death. However, they also believed some spirits could remain or return to haunt the living, especially when their death had been unnatural, their bodily remains had not been properly buried, or their spirit had unfinished business among the living. Homer, a Greek poet and author of the epic tales *The Iliad* and *The Odyssey*, wrote about his characters' encounters with ghosts in both works. In these epics, ghosts often appeared to warn of future events or to note that their human remains had not been given a proper burial. Ulysses, the main character of *The Odyssey*, describes one such meeting with the ghost of a warrior friend who had died in battle: "The first ghost that came was that of my comrade Elpenor, for he had not yet been laid beneath the Earth. We had left his body unwaked and unburied . . . for we had had too much else to do."[7] The term *unwaked* meant that Elpenor had not been given a proper wake, or funeral, and therefore was unable to rest peacefully in the afterlife.

> "The pyramids were said to be haunted by living spirits who would keep out all intruders."[6]
>
> —Egyptologists Robert M. Schoch and Robert Aquinas McNally.

Like the ancient Greeks, the people of ancient Rome believed ghosts of the dead could show themselves to and even communicate with the living. In fact, some ancient Romans wrote descriptions of what they believed were true hauntings, not merely parts of fictional stories. One account of a supposedly real haunted house was written by a Roman politician named Pliny the Younger in the first century. Pliny's account, discovered among a collection of his personal letters, tells of a house plagued by a restless spirit. At night, the ghost terrified the home's inhabitants with noises Pliny described as being similar to the rattling of chains. "The wretched occupants would spend fearful nights awake in terror," he wrote.

"The house was therefore deserted . . . but it was advertised as being to let or for sale in case someone was found who knew nothing of its evil reputation."[8]

One night a philosopher who had heard of the house's reputation visited it and followed the ghost into the garden, where it pointed at the ground and then disappeared. The next day the remains of a human body that had been wrapped in chains were unearthed at the spot where the ghost had pointed. Pliny's letter said that once the body was properly buried, the ghost never returned—a concept common to many tales of ghosts and hauntings today.

Intercontinental Haunts

Stories and accounts of ghosts and hauntings were not limited to the continents of Africa and Europe. Ancient cultures in Asia and the Americas believed in hauntings as well. The Chinese believed spirits of people who had died could return, especially if the death had involved a battle or drowning or when the body had not received a proper burial. The Chinese also thought spirits could return to seek justice for wrongdoing. In the fifth century, Chinese philosopher and religious leader Mo Ti argued that ghosts and hauntings should logically be considered real as long as the people describing encounters with them were believable. "He reasoned that when people tell of how a certain machine operates with which one is not acquainted, or how certain people behave or speak in a land they have never been to, one should accept what they say if their report seems credible and if they, themselves, seem reliable witnesses," says historian Joshua J. Mark. "As ancient historical accounts, as well as contemporary reports of his time, contained references to ghosts, they should be accepted as a reality in the same way one recognized established history and news reports of the day."[9] Modern believers in ghosts and hauntings often use similar logic to justify their acceptance of strange phenomena.

The people of the Americas, too, developed their own concepts of ghosts and hauntings beginning in ancient times. The Navajo Indians, who historically lived in modern-day Utah, Arizona, and New Mexico, believed that people who were not at

A Haunting in India

India is home to one of the world's oldest surviving cultures. Many of India's people readily accept the existence of ghosts, which they call *bhoots*, and believe in haunted sites. Bhangarh Fort, near the city of Delhi, is among the most notorious haunted places in India. Built on a hillside in 1573, Bhangarh's stone buildings are said to have been cursed centuries ago by a holy man named Baba Balnath, who gave permission to construct the town only if its buildings never overshadowed his own home on the hillside. According to legend, Baba Balnath cursed the town when its residents built a castle tall enough to cast the shadow he had forbidden.

People have claimed frightful phenomena have occurred at the site ever since. In 1783 residents abandoned Bhangarh and moved their town away. Today rumors persist that nobody who stays within the boundaries of the fort past sundown will emerge alive the next day. Many might say the story is a myth, but the Archaeological Survey of India, a government agency, has made it illegal to cross the boundaries of the fort between sunset and sunrise. This suggests that the stories perhaps should be taken seriously.

peace when they died or who were not properly buried could return to torment the living. "After the spirit is gone there is something evil about the body which none of the Navajos understand, and of which they are afraid,"[10] a Navajo medicine man explained to researcher Franc Johnson Newcomb when she lived with and studied the Navajo in the mid-1900s. Indians who lived in the Pacific Northwest also believed that spirits of the dead could haunt the living. Some groups buried their dead on islands in the Columbia River, far from their own villages, because they believed that spirits of the deceased could not cross the water and would thus remain trapped in burial grounds.

All over the world, since human beings first began to tell, write, and preserve their own history, their stories have included ghosts and hauntings. The similarities between beliefs about the nature of spirits and why they haunt certain places have long fascinated historians. "A ghost needs to be given specific physical attributes or non-physical abilities in order for people to imagine that there exists 'something,'" says historian Mu-Chou Poo, "and . . . a place needs to be identified where the ghost can dwell."[11]

Hauntings Through the Centuries

Belief in ghosts, evil spirits, curses, witchcraft, and other frightful explanations for everything from solar eclipses to illness continued to be common throughout the Middle Ages, the period from the fifth to the fifteenth century. The early years of this era are often called the Dark Ages because many people, especially in Europe, lacked a formal education, were poor, and had little formal or scientific understanding of the world. Deadly feuds over land and power were common between kings and between wealthy nobles; rulers built and lived in huge stone castles. Castles stood for centuries, and various violent or mysterious deaths took place in most of them over the years. Features like dark, drafty passageways and underground dungeons made these massive fortresses frequent sites for ghostly sightings.

> "A ghost needs to be given specific physical attributes or non-physical abilities in order for people to imagine that there exists 'something' . . . a place needs to be identified where the ghost can dwell."[11]
>
> —Historian Mu-Chou Poo.

Lacking knowledge of science and real-world explanations for many phenomena, people during the Middle Ages readily believed in the supernatural and were easily convinced that any place where strange sounds or sights occurred was haunted by the spirits of the dead. Many such beliefs have survived into modern times, even in defiance of logical explanations that have been offered for the phenomena. Many of the castles that still stand today—especially in Great Britain, a country with a rich history of recordkeeping and storytelling—are associated with centuries of folklore about spirits and hauntings. "There are few towns in England that do not boast a bevy of spirits raised from the dead—to warn, to punish, to frighten, or simply to remind," says religion and history researcher and writer Charles A. Coulombe, "but it is in the castles and palaces of the wealthy and renowned that they are most reliably to be found."[12]

From the fourteenth to the seventeenth century in Europe, the Middle Ages gradually gave way to the Renaissance, a period of revived learning. During this era many people embraced education and eagerly studied the discoveries and philosophies of the

The strange sounds that echoed through the dark and drafty passageways of medieval castles were often attributed to the spirits of the dead. Ghostly sightings were also common among those who occupied or visited these structures.

Haunted White House

If spirits do linger in places linked to important periods of their lives, then the White House—home to every American president and first lady since 1800—has likely accumulated a few spirits. Many presidents, first ladies, visitors, and family members have in fact reported strange phenomena in the presidential estate. Abraham Lincoln, president in the 1860s when paranormal investigation was becoming a popular American pastime, reportedly held séances at the White House with his wife, Mary, in an attempt to communicate with their deceased young son. Winston Churchill, former prime minister of Great Britain, is said to have seen Lincoln's ghost during a stay at the White House and refused ever to spend the night there again. Many people have reported seeing Dolley Madison, first lady from 1809 to 1817, in the Rose Garden, which she had planted. Ronald Reagan reported that his family members saw strange spirits in the house and that his dog, Rex, barked at invisible things and refused to enter the Lincoln Bedroom. Presidents and prime ministers are elected to positions of authority because a majority of their citizens trust them to be realistic, level-headed leaders, so claims of hauntings by people like Reagan and Churchill are compelling.

past, especially the work of the ancient Greeks and Romans. Inevitably Renaissance learners encountered tales of ghosts and hauntings among the ancient classical works of Greek and Roman philosophers, poets, and scholars. Many of these accounts seemed similar to what was occurring in European locations that were believed to be haunted.

Hauntings were a common theme in Renaissance art and literature. William Shakespeare, arguably the most celebrated playwright of all time, wrote at least thirty-seven plays, many of which featured ghosts. In *Hamlet*, one of Shakespeare's best-known plays, the spirit of Hamlet's murdered father presents itself to Hamlet to ask for revenge. A scene in the play *Macbeth* features a floating knife leading the title character to commit a murderous deed. In *Julius Caesar*, the spirit of the slain Caesar appears to his former friend and companion Brutus, warning of Brutus's own looming death. The belief that some spirits lingered after death—especially if they were victims of violence, murder, or foul play—was as common during the Renaissance as it had been during the time of the ancient Greeks and Romans. Therefore, Shakespeare's audiences in the 1500s and 1600s would have accepted the possibility of such ghostly sightings.

People's widespread belief in spirits during the Middle Ages and the Renaissance was often linked to religion. Spirits could be portrayed as angelic and positive, but more often they were associated with evil. Unexplained phenomena attributed to ghosts or hauntings were sometimes also linked with specific people who were accused of communicating with or summoning the dead. In an era ruled by superstition and devout religious beliefs, rumors and accusations of dabbling in the supernatural could quickly give way to public outrage or panic.

People associated with the site of an unexplained phenomenon like a reported ghost sighting became targets of public fear and suspicion. Witch hunts, the search for people—mainly women—believed to have evil supernatural powers, occurred throughout Europe in the 1500s and 1600s. Anyone suspected of communicating with the dead could be labeled a witch, and the penalty was typically death by means such as hanging or being burned alive. These incidents were not limited to Europe. Across the Atlantic Ocean in the newly established British colonies of North America, witch scares swept several towns of the colony that became modern-day Massachusetts. The Salem Witch Trials, as they are known, led to the execution of twenty people accused of being witches or sorcerers. It is one of history's worst examples of public hysteria caused by belief in and fear of unexplainable phenomena that in modern times might be called hauntings.

Bringing Hauntings into the Light

The Renaissance in Europe was followed by the Age of Enlightenment, also known as the Age of Reason. During this period, which lasted from the mid-1600s to about 1800, Europeans came to believe that reasonable scientific explanations could be found for anything. Superstition, fear, and the tendency to shun unexplained phenomena like ghosts and haunted places was replaced by curiosity about them and a determination to find a logical scientific explanation. During the 1800s in the United States and Europe—especially Great Britain and France—investigations of haunted places and attempts to summon and communicate with ghosts became a popular fad. People began to claim that they had special talents for communicating with spirits. They called themselves mediums—people who act as a bridge between the world of the dead and the world of the living.

By the mid-nineteenth century, seeking out ghostly phenomena was a popular pastime. Groups of people, often as a form of entertainment after dinner parties, took part in séances. "In the séance sessions, a group of like-minded believers and the curious sat around a table, holding or touching . . . hands for positive energy vibrations, while a selected medium (the spirit world go-between) would direct or answer questions to and from the spirit world,"[13] says Larry Dreller, a practicing medium. Participants in séances often asked for physical signs that the spirit was present, such as for the spirit to knock on or to physically move the table. Many supposedly true accounts emerged of unexplained knocking or of dining tables being tipped over or shoved across the room during séances.

Talking boards also became very popular during this period as a way to communicate with ghosts in one's home. Talking boards had the letters of the alphabet written on them. A small group of at least two people would gather around the board and place their fingers lightly on a planchette, a small teardrop-shaped piece of wood placed on the board. Someone would ask a question out loud, and the planchette would reportedly move to point to letters and spell out a response. In 1891, the Kennard Novelty Company of Baltimore, Maryland, began producing and selling a new version of the talking board called the Ouija board; supposedly its inventors used the board to ask it what its name should be and it spelled out the letters "ouija." This new style of talking board not only had the letters of the alphabet but the numbers one through

The Ouija board supposedly spells out answers to questions asked by users who are eager to communicate with the dead. This device supplanted mediums as the only means of such communication.

nine, the words *yes* and *no* for quicker answers to questions, and the greetings *hello* and *goodbye*. Ouija boards, users believed, made it easier for people to communicate with spirits because it eliminated the need for a medium.

Separating Fact from Fiction

The popularity of attempting to communicate with ghosts in the nineteenth century, especially in buildings people believed were haunted, also exposed many mediums or ghost experts as frauds. Cameras (invented in the mid-1800s and available to the public by the 1890s) were used to take photographs of what seemed to be strange ghostly phenomena. At some point, however, it was proved that film could be deliberately altered to show seemingly strange things like faces or hands emerging from clouds of mist. Doubters also claimed that talking boards were probably being deliberately manipulated by one of the people in a group and that tables were being shaken or tilted by the knees of the medium or even a séance participant.

Investigations of hauntings became a popular pastime during the Age of Reason, but they brought no reasonable explanations to the peculiar phenomena associated with haunted houses. If anything, people who prided themselves on being reasonable came to see such paranormal investigations as hoaxes. Yet investigations continued well past this period. In the 1910s and early 1920s Harry Houdini, one of the most famous magicians and illusionists of all time, developed a keen interest in the possibility that he might contact the spirit of his dead mother. He enlisted the help of numerous self-described mediums only to find that they relied on illusions, much the same as he did, to fool their audiences. Houdini methodically debunked numerous mediums. His efforts did much to fuel doubts that ghosts of the deceased could be contacted, if such spirits even did exist.

Houdini was not the first to bring a fact-based approach to studies of the paranormal. In 1852, the Society for Psychical Research (SPR) was founded in London with the goal of investigating supposed spiritual, paranormal, and unexplained phenomena using scientific methods. The society conducted scientific experiments, approached strange phenomena with the idea that a reasonable explanation could be found, and even published its studies and findings in a scholarly journal. These activities launched a new trend of scientific inquiry into phenomena like haunted houses that lasted through the twentieth century. "Phenomena could be observed and experienced by everyone," says history professor Sofie Lachapelle. "It would be a different kind of science. It would be accessible and inclusive: an open enterprise."[14] The SPR is still active today and has a branch in the United States—the American Society for Psychical Research. This and similar organizations developed with the goal of applying science to unexplained phenomena, including haunted houses. They sought to separate hoaxes and sensationalism from real experiences.

An Ancient Belief in a Modern World

The fascination with ghosts and haunted places has not diminished with time, but then, neither has skepticism about such events. Technology can be and often is used to create the illusion of evidence where none exists. Many skeptics also say that the widespread notion of a haunted house as being a large, run-down mansion has conditioned people to imagine strange phenomena in any place they perceive as creepy, even if no such phenomena actually occur. Just because a building is old does not mean it harbors restless spirits of deceased people, even if it has been the site of one or more deaths over the years. There is also no logical reason why a brand-new home could not be haunted as readily as an old one. Still, the notion that older houses are the haunted ones overwhelmingly persists in society, suggesting that beliefs may be based more on widespread hearsay than on logic or facts.

Just the same, many people refuse to be deterred by skepticism and hold fast to their belief that some houses and other buildings are truly haunted by spirits or some sort of paranormal forces. The quest to capture scientific proof of such phenomena continues, but perhaps the most compelling evidence takes the form of eyewitness testimonies from people who claim to have experienced strange phenomena. More than any other factor, these accounts seem to compel many people to seek out places that are rumored to be haunted so they can try to witness a frightening incident themselves.

Chapter 2

Encounters with Haunted Houses

"I can honestly say that I've seen things that baffled me, experienced things that surprised me, learned things that gave me pause, and above all, acquired a new understanding of possibilities that has altered my life. Something is out there."

—Katherine Ramsland, forensic psychologist and paranormal author/investigator.

Katherine Ramsland, *Ghost: Investigating the Other Side*. New York: St. Martin's Press, 2001, p. xiv.

"For many, the only real ghosts that exist are the ones that haunt the insides of their heads."

—Paranormal expert and author Sam Baltrusis.

Sam Baltrusis, *Ghosts of Cambridge: Haunts of Harvard Square and Beyond*. Charleston, SC: Haunted America, 2013, p. 13.

If ever there were a stereotypical haunted house, a house on 222nd Street in the Laurelton suburb of Queens, New York, is it. The two-and-three-quarter-story Victorian-style house has weathered siding, tilting porches, boarded-up windows, and padlocked gates in the rusty chain-link fence that separates the house from the street. The run-down appearance of the house suggests both age and neglect. The roof sags. The walls slope. Some of the windows are broken. From the look of the place, the inside must be similarly unkempt—dusty and creaky, dim and dingy, possibly with rotting floorboards that pose a real danger should they give way. A large "X" painted on the porch poses a warning to keep out. Such houses seem to hide secrets. They seem to harbor ghosts. Neighbors have long wondered about the house, which has gained a reputation as being haunted.

The world is filled with buildings that possess similar traits. Impossible to ignore, they collect rumors and stories as readily as dust in their corners, especially if anyone is known (or even suspected) to have died in the house in a violent way. "No matter where you go, in every town, village, or city across America, there is always one location that is considered haunted or has some ghostly legend attached to it," says mental health counselor and psychical researcher Greg Jenkins. "The thought of ghosts in creepy old mansions feeds the imagination."[15] Some communities shun their local hauntings. Others embrace them and even turn them into sources of public amusement. As tales of people's encounters with such places accumulate, they feed an age-old human obsession with the still unanswered question of whether haunted houses really exist.

> "The thought of ghosts in creepy old mansions feeds the imagination."[15]
>
> —Mental health counselor and psychical researcher Greg Jenkins.

Hauntings of Legend

Many buildings rumored to be haunted are private residences, and trespassers are warned to stay out. These creaky-looking abodes are usually viewed from a distance and gain only local notoriety. Other reportedly haunted places are public, or at least have become so as a result of their haunted reputation. Such buildings attract tourists, often by the thousands, all hoping to experience for themselves what other people claim to have felt, heard, or seen.

The older the building and the more sordid its past, the more haunted it is generally expected to be. Believers in ghosts tend to accept that human spirits are more likely to linger in a place that was important to them during life or where they met an untimely end, such as through illness, murder, or betrayal. Parapsychologist and ghost hunter Loyd Auerbach describes the phenomenon of haunting as "some kind of environmental recording of events and people . . . the house, building, or land somehow records its history, with more emotion-laden events and experiences coming through louder and stronger."[16] The older the structure, the more likely it has housed people whose spirits may feel attached to it. A lengthy history also provides a greater share of the stories of tragedy, heartbreak, and revenge believed to surround restless spirits that are bound to an earthly place.

Europe is filled with many such places. Castles, designed to loom imposingly over the surrounding countryside, have been sites of war, punishment, and royal betrayals on the continent for centuries. Drafty, dim, and filled with mazelike passageways and lonely echoes, castles are places where it is easy to imagine being watched or even followed by unseen residents. The Tower of London is one of the world's oldest and most famous places with a haunted history. Built on the banks of the Thames River by William the Conqueror in 1066, it has been the site of many violent and troubling incidents during the past millennium. The tower was at times used as a prison and became a site of torture and death. Three English queens were among those executed at the Tower of London over the years, most famously Anne Boleyn, the second wife of King Henry VIII. Anne was beheaded at the Tower of London on May 19, 1536, after Henry accused her of treason and other crimes, accusations he invented because he wanted to marry someone else. Ever since, the vision of a lady dressed in sixteenth-century fashion, believed to be the spirit of Anne, is said to appear every May 19. Dozens of people claim to have seen her.

> "The house, building, or land somehow records its history, with more emotion-laden events and experiences coming through louder and stronger."[16]
>
> —Parapsychologist and ghost hunter Loyd Auerbach.

The apparition of Anne Boleyn is among many other paranormal incidents reported by staff members and visitors to this site over the centuries. "There have been reports of 54 separate hauntings at the Tower, from full-blown apparitions to some supernaturally unpleasant smells,"[17] says British paranormal historian Leo Ruickbie. Accounts of ghostly sightings believed to be the remnants of various people imprisoned in or executed at the castle are not the only incidents reported there. Over the years some tower employees and visitors have claimed they feel

Over the centuries, visitors to the Chapel Royal at the Tower of London (pictured) have claimed to see or hear the wandering spirit of Anne Boleyn. Boleyn, the second wife of Henry VIII, was imprisoned and beheaded there in the 1500s.

squeezed or crushed by a heavy weight in certain rooms. Others have said they smell the sometimes overpowering odor of a woman's perfume. The Tower of London's long-standing history of violence, betrayal, and unpleasantness has imprinted it with rumors of haunted activity that are all but impossible to dispel.

Frightened Families

Most of the specters at the Tower of London fall into a category known as residual ghosts. These are spirits that seem to linger on after a tragedy; they interact with the space more for their own memories than because they care — or are even aware — that any living people can see them. The energy of such spirits, many paranormal investigators believe, is said to imprint on a place but often has no real purpose. "In some cases, it would seem obvious that the spirits are able to see, hear, and communicate with the living," says paranormal author Keith Grossl. "But in the case of residual hauntings, the spirits involved seem completely unaware of our living presence."[18]

Most notorious hauntings, on the other hand, become legendary not because they are eerie but because they are downright frightening. Some houses are said to be haunted by one or more presences that want to be noticed — and they make sure that anyone who sets foot in the house knows of their existence. Such spirits may go to great lengths to frighten or even harm human visitors or residents, supposedly either to chase them away or because these spirits simply seem to enjoy creating terror.

One such home in America is a three-story colonial-style residence built in the 1920s in the town of Amityville, New York. In 1974, twenty-three-year-old Ronald DeFeo Jr. murdered his mother, father, and all four of his siblings in the house. A year later, George and Kathy Lutz purchased the home despite knowing of its violent past. In December 1975 they and their three children moved in. Less than a month later, in mid-January 1976, the Lutz family fled the home. They described strange and terrifying incidents such as hearing footsteps overhead when no one was upstairs or seeing glowing red eyes that seemed to look in the windows at them. Kathy reported being touched and pushed by an unseen presence. The children claimed they were awakened when their beds began to slide around on the floor in the middle of the night. The family said they experienced mood and behavior changes, too.

After the Lutzes moved out, the house became a magnet for paranormal investigators. The Lutz family's experiences were published in a 1977 book titled *The Amityville Horror*. The book spawned numerous movies and documentaries, many of which were found to have highly exaggerated the facts and included many details that were purely fictional. Skeptics like Joe Nickell have characterized the Lutzes' story as falling far short of convincing: "The bottom line is that . . . it was a hoax, or is, simply, at best, a matter that's not proven," he says. "And that's not very good for America's most famous haunted house."[19] However, George and Kathy Lutz, both of whom passed lie detector tests about their experiences, maintained throughout their lives that the haunting was real.

Murderous Mansions

People's fascination with the tale of the Amityville haunting is mirrored in other buildings known to have been sites of ghastly deaths. On the corner of Royal and Governor Nichols Streets in

Tombs of Stone

Since the time of the ancient Greeks, people have believed human spirits attach to porous materials such as rocks, bricks, and concrete. This theory could help explain why so many old buildings, most of which are made of stone or bricks (rather than wood, which decomposes over time), are reportedly haunted by many generations of trapped human spirits.

The idea that rocks can trap ghosts is also supported by a history of strange phenomena occurring in underground caves. Mammoth Cave in Kentucky is one such cave reported to be haunted. In 1925 a man named Floyd Collins was caught in a tight crevice in the cave when a rock fell on his ankle and prevented him from escaping. For more than two weeks, friends, family, and rescue workers attempted various methods to rescue Collins. Their efforts failed, and he died in the cave. Ever since, cave visitors have claimed to experience such phenomena as the sound of a male voice begging for help. If rocks can hold troubled spirits, the ghost of Floyd Collins may still be trapped in its stone crypt in Kentucky.

The LaLaurie mansion in New Orleans, Louisiana (pictured), is said to be haunted by the spirits of slaves who were tortured to death by one of the building's former owners. Unexplainable sounds including shouting and doors slamming have convinced visitors and staff that the house is haunted.

New Orleans sits the stately LaLaurie Mansion. Its history is as unnerving and notorious as that of the famous haunted home of Amityville. The three-story mansion, built in the early 1830s in downtown New Orleans, was home to Louis and Delphine LaLaurie. The couple owned numerous household slaves, and Delphine had a reputation for abusing them. She once chased a young slave with a whip all the way upstairs and out onto the roof. The girl fell to her death, and Delphine had the body buried on the property to cover up the incident. In 1834 the mansion caught fire; rescue workers and fire crews were horrified to discover seven slaves still alive and chained to the walls with spiked iron collars around their necks. The stories the slaves told of torture at the hands of their cruel mistress were so horrifying that they enraged the people of New Orleans, forcing Louis and Delphine to flee the city to save their own lives.

The LaLaurie Mansion, remodeled and historically preserved, is widely reported to be haunted by the spirits of slaves who were tortured to death inside its walls. "This house has mesmerized people for nearly two hundred years," say historian Victoria Cosner Love and author Lorelei Shannon. "After the LaLaurie estate sold the house, a long and bumpy ride of tenants, businesses and private owners paraded through and were usually driven out by the alleged hauntings and happenings. The history of the house is a testament to the power of the LaLaurie legend."[20]

Visitors and maintenance workers have described the unexplained sounds of people shouting and doors slamming as well as of being touched by unseen hands. Passersby have reported seeing ghostly faces looking out at the street from upstairs windows. The home became the setting of the television drama *American Horror Story: Coven* in 2011, starring actress Kathy Bates as Madame LaLaurie. Its connection with the entertainment industry is strengthened by the fact that film actor Nicolas Cage owned the mansion from 2006 to 2009.

Getting Close to Restless Spirits

The violent events known to have taken place inside the walls of the Amityville house and the LaLaurie Mansion have inspired filmmakers, television producers, and novelists to retell the dramatic and frightening tales. They often take liberties with the facts in order to terrify their viewers and readers and heighten the popularity of their books or movies. Haunted houses naturally accumulate both rumors and fame, spawning not just a vibrant film genre but an active branch of the tourism industry as well.

One home with an infamous reputation is the Lizzie Borden Bed and Breakfast in Fall River, Massachusetts, the site of one of the most famous murder cases in American history. In 1892, Andrew Borden was found dead on a downstairs sofa, having been hacked to death with a hatchet. His wife, Abby, was killed in an upstairs bedroom in the same fashion. Thirty-two-year-old Lizzie, Andrew's daughter and Abby's stepdaughter, still lived at home along with her sister, Emma. Lizzie was the one who found her father's body. Police immediately suspected she had committed both the murders. (Emma was out of town at the time.) During a widely publicized murder trial, Lizzie was ultimately acquitted of the brutal crimes, which were never solved.

The Bordens' home has since been restored to resemble as closely as possible what it looked like during the era of the murders, including an exact replica of the sofa where Andrew Borden was murdered. The building is now a museum and also a bed and breakfast where guests can stay overnight. Daring visitors can sleep in the very room where Abby Borden's body was found. Many ghostly experiences have been reported in the building, including chilly breezes and the sensation of being nudged or touched. Some guests over the years have experienced such strange things that they have fled the home in the middle of the night. Nevertheless, the place is so popular among thrill seekers that it requires reservations, sometimes months in advance, especially if someone wants to book a room on August 4, the anniversary of the murders.

Transforming places like the Borden house into tourist attractions has become a profitable industry, and the more notorious a home's ghostly reputation, the more popular it seems to become. "Attitudes towards ghosts and hauntings vary greatly from place to place," say paranormal investigators Joel Martin and William J. Birnes, but "many communities have seen the wisdom of embracing ghosts and the tourists they attract."[21]

> "Many communities have seen the wisdom of embracing ghosts and the tourists they attract."[21]
>
> —Paranormal investigators Joel Martin and William J. Birnes.

Tourists flock to places like the Winchester Mystery House in San Jose, California, a home built by American firearms heiress Sarah Winchester over the course of several decades. Widely believed to be crazy, the widow ordered increasingly peculiar features to be added to her sprawling 160-room, 10,000-square-foot estate, including numerous secret passageways and forty-seven flights of stairs, some of which dead-end into walls. Mrs. Winchester is believed to have designed the home in part to elude the ghosts she reportedly believed were haunting her—the spirits of men who had been killed by Winchester rifles. Construction workers and servants at the home have described many creepy incidents such as rattling doorknobs, the sound of

Ghost or Hoax?

In November 1974 police in Bridgeport, Connecticut, responded to a distress call from a terrified family living in a small house on Lindley Street. The residence was in chaos. Police officers and firefighters who responded to the scene saw furniture and television sets being picked up and set back down by some unseen force. The homeowners, Gerald and Laura Goodin, had a school-aged child, an adopted daughter named Marcia. A police officer reported that at one point, he witnessed an unseen force slam Marcia against a wall.

Word of the apparent haunting spread rapidly, and soon Lindley Street was crowded with spectators hoping to glimpse strange events. Within two days, the incident was international news, and the crowd numbered in the thousands. For the most part, only people permitted to enter the home witnessed unexplained events, but dozens of them reported baffling phenomena. Many were police and emergency responders who regularly witnessed shocking things but said they had never seen anything like the forces afflicting that home.

On the third day after the strange events started, the Bridgeport chief of police released a statement that the entire incident had been a hoax. Forty years later, in 2014, Bridgeport native William J. Hall published a book based on careful research about the incident, claiming it cannot be entirely dismissed as imaginary. "There were over 100 witnesses," he says. "This is one of the most witnessed hauntings in history."

Quoted in Fausto Giovanny Pinto, "Author Recounts Story of Haunted Bridgeport House," *Connecticut Post*, October 4, 2014. www.ctpost.com.

screws being backed out of the walls, and lights spontaneously turning on throughout an entire floor of the seven-story building.

Mrs. Winchester died in 1922, and construction on the home halted so abruptly that some carpenters left nails only halfway

A ghostly image plays piano at the Winchester Mystery House in San Jose, California. The former owner is thought to have built the house with secret passageways and dead-end turns to elude the ghosts that haunted her.

hammered into walls. Shortly thereafter, the home was opened to tourists hoping to witness for themselves some of the haunted lore of the place. "The Winchester house has been a tourist attraction since 1923," says historian Mary Jo Ignoffo. "The gangly house is touted by huge red-and-black billboards along California's highways and beyond, luring the curious with a silhouetted house superimposed by a human skull. The signs suggest that visitors may encounter an apparition from another realm."[22] It is one of the most famous examples of modern society's fascination with the idea of a haunted house.

Televised Presences

Television shows geared toward the investigation of haunted buildings have added to the fame of locations said to host supernatural presences. Numerous shows have become popular in recent years, such as the Travel Channel's *Ghost Adventures* and the SyFy Channel's *Ghost Hunters*. Although these shows differ in the types of investigators they bring into a location—usually a mixture of psychics, skeptics, and experienced ghost hunters—they tend to follow a similar format. They explain the history of the building and any strange events, murders, or historical tragedies that have happened there and that could potentially be the source of a haunting. Then investigators spend time in the building, generally at night, to attempt to record or experience peculiar phenomena. The finished shows, which last from thirty to sixty minutes when later aired on television, usually include some kind of wrap-up statement indicating that based on their findings, the investigators cannot prove the location is haunted, but they cannot rule out the possibility either.

Such shows have helped establish a renewed sense of fascination with the paranormal. In addition, they have reinforced widespread ideas about signs of a haunting. The shows are often criticized by believers in haunted houses for giving the impression that a variety of otherwise explainable phenomena could be signs of a haunting or that spending one night in a haunted place will yield plenty of ghostly experiences. Paranormal investigators often point out that patience and time are required to study hauntings and that rarely do numerous and obvious signs accumulate in a single night. "There are plenty of people wanting to do exactly what they see on TV," says paranormal writer and investigator Deonna Kelli Sayed. "Group culture now defines how we access the paranormal in terms of investigation—and it is far more work than most realize."[23] Despite often being criticized for misrepresenting paranormal investigation, television shows have made ghostly phenomena a mainstream experience and allowed more people than ever before to see what an encounter with a haunted house might really be like.

Turning Skeptics into Believers

People who believe in haunted houses rarely base their beliefs solely on rumors or televised programs about hauntings. Many say they have personally experienced paranormal phenomena that, for them, have no other explanation. Ed Pearce, a news reporter in Nevada, had an experience in Virginia City, a historical Nevada mining town where numerous buildings are reportedly haunted. "I'm a confirmed skeptic, agnostic about all things paranormal," Pearce says. "I'd never seen anything I couldn't explain."[24]

That was before he and a group of paranormal investigators spent part of a night in a former Civil War–era hospital. While there, he says, a motion detector hidden in a stuffed teddy bear flashed unexpectedly after one of the investigators asked whether there were any ghosts in the room. At first, Pearce says, he merely found the phenomenon odd, but "Viewing the night vision video a week later, I saw something else. . . . The auto focus on the camera suddenly begins searching and something coming from the direction of the bear whisks by my head." Pearce, who has built a career out of reporting facts, admits he cannot easily declare the experience as imaginary. "All I know is I've now seen something I can't explain and I'm not sure how this life-long skeptic should feel about that."[25]

Many believers in haunted houses are not reporters or television personalities at all. They are everyday people who insist haunted houses are real because they claim to have lived in one. Darlene McCall owns and has lived in a century-old farmhouse in Nova Scotia, Canada, for more than three decades. She claims to have experienced countless frightening experiences in her home ranging from being touched and pulled on the basement steps to feeling as if someone is sitting on her chest when she is in her bed at night. Like many people who say they have experienced hauntings, she seems wary of other people's criticism; she silently endured decades of torment before finally deciding to publicly share her story. "I always thought right from the start that there is something watching me, but I didn't dare open my mouth and say anything because I thought people would think I was nuts,"[26] she says.

Reluctance to admit that they believe in ghosts may keep many people from speaking about their experiences. It is possible that many—even a majority—of stories about hauntings happen in private residences and are never publicized. Fear of being criticized by skeptics could silence many people who have experienced strange and unexplainable phenomena. This presses many scientifically minded investigators to seek actual, physical proof of hauntings that will validate people's claims. Such proof could help set at ease the minds of believers who fear being ridiculed if they share their personal experiences with hauntings and would demonstrate once and for all that ghostly activity does occur in haunted places.

Chapter 3

The Study of Haunted Houses

"Curiously, while debunkers and skeptics insist that hundreds of millions of paranormal experiences are worthless as evidence, in the criminal justice system, one witness is sometimes sufficient to convict someone of a crime. So we are willing to take the word of a single individual in a court of law, while at the same time, ignoring multitudes of witnesses to the paranormal."

—Paranormal investigators Joel Martin and William J. Birnes.

Joel Martin and William J. Birnes, *The Haunting of Twenty-First-Century America*. New York: Forge, 2013, p. 74.

"Concerning the psychic anecdote, the story about a ghost, apparition, or meaningful coincidence, one point cannot be stressed too strongly: there is no such thing as a reliable, objective informant, regardless of how upright, socially eminent, or educated the informant might be."

—Psychologists Leonard Zusne and Warren H. Jones.

Leonard Zusne and Warren H. Jones, *Anomalistic Psychology: A Study of Magical Thinking*. New York: Psychology Press, 2014, p. 226.

Belief in haunted houses is often based on something called anecdotal evidence. Anecdotes are stories, and anecdotal evidence of the paranormal is therefore a story (or multiple stories) of people's experiences with a certain phenomenon. If just one person reports peculiar experiences in a particular house, the anecdotal evidence could have many explanations. Perhaps the person has an overactive imagination or mistook certain explainable sounds or sights as being supernatural. On the other hand, if many people tell about peculiar things happening in the same house, the anecdotal evidence of a haunting becomes stronger, especially if these people describe similar or identical phenomena, have never met or spoken to each other, and visit the house at completely different times. Anecdotal evidence can be very convincing. "Many millions of so-called psi [paranormal] anecdotes form a substantial body of evidence that something is occurring that should not be ignored," say paranormal investigators Joel Martin and William J. Birnes. "Equally curious is why innumerable psi incidents bear striking similarities to each other, regardless of where they take place or to whom. The commonalities suggest that something more than imagination is at work."[27]

Numerous firsthand accounts of haunted places around the world describing similar phenomena have led ghost researchers to develop and use particular instruments and methods for studying and recording unexplained occurrences. Those who use technology to study haunted houses have come closer than ever before to showing that the phenomena in reportedly haunted buildings have consistent and measurable characteristics that may provide true evidence of hauntings.

> "Innumerable psi [paranormal] incidents bear striking similarities to each other, regardless of where they take place or to whom. The commonalities suggest that something more than imagination is at work."[27]
>
> —*Paranormal investigators Joel Martin and William J. Birnes.*

Moans, Groans, and Other Ghostly Sounds

Unexplained noises are one of the first and most noticeable phenomena that indicate a house might be haunted. Noises such as footsteps or the sound of objects being dragged across the floor; doors or cupboards opening on creaky hinges or slamming closed; thumps or knocking sounds on walls or furniture; and whispers, voices, or laughter when no one else is in the room or building are all associated with hauntings. A person who hears sounds such as these might once have had difficulty proving exactly what he or she heard. For the most part, until the twentieth century, people who claimed they experienced such phenomena had to hope that other people would believe them.

When American inventor Thomas Edison created a device in the mid-1800s that could record and play back voices based on sound waves moving through the air, the public immediately seized the technique as a possible way to capture the words of the dead. "Voice recording seemed capable of summoning from their graves even those who had long perished,"[28] says science writer Philip Ball. Paranormal investigators have used this technology ever since to try to capture evidence of ghostly sounds.

Many improvements were made to Edison's primitive recording machine over the years. In the 1960s and 1970s, small, portable, and affordable devices called cassette tape recorders became popular for recording everything from music to human voices. These devices used disposable, re-recordable, and interchangeable plastic tape cassettes. They could record nearby sounds and play them back with the press of a button. Although they had disadvantages, such as a tendency to capture fuzzy recordings because of the mechanical noise of the strip of magnetic tape being wound and unwound around its reels within the cassette, cassette recorders became very popular devices for the investigation of haunted houses. They could capture evidence of voices or sounds that witnesses could play back to convince other people of what they had heard.

Continuous improvements were made to sound-recording technology over the next decades. Most modern investigators of haunted buildings use digital recording devices, which were invented in the 1990s and transform sounds into a unique code of numbers (digits) that can then be decoded and played back. Digital recorders have many advantages over cassette recorders. They obtain much clearer sound, because audio tapes themselves make noises that could interfere with other sounds during a recording. Digital devices can also record dozens or even hundreds of hours of audio.

Another advantage of digital sound files is that they can be enhanced with computer software programs that reduce background noise, amplify specific sounds or aspects of a sound, change the pitch (the highness or lowness) of the sound, and speed up or slow down the recording. Digital recorders also can

Modern-day ghost hunters use an array of devices for gathering evidence of a ghostly presence. Among these (from left to right) are meters that measure electromagnetic energy, digital audio recorders, and a device that measures room temperatures and electromagnetic fields.

be small enough to fit into a writing pen or even a wristwatch, making them easy for paranormal investigators to carry with them wherever they believe they might hear haunted phenomena.

Some investigators prefer to use both cassette recorders and digital ones because they claim each type can capture different kinds of sounds. "Champions of analogue [tape] recorders say that there is something about the way sound is recorded onto analogue tape that lends itself to be easily manipulated by the 'spirit world,' which apparently is something that cannot be achieved as easily on digital formats," say paranormal investigators Mark Rosney, Rob Bethell, and Jebby Robinson. However, they add, "Since most digital devices are solid state (no moving parts), they do not suffer from the problems that can plague tape recorders, such as mechanical failure and internal noise generated by the recorder's moving parts."[29] By using both types of recording devices in an investigation, investigators may obtain a wider variety of results.

A Higher Degree of Ghostly Studies

The scientific community generally rejects the investigation of haunted buildings as science. It is often described, instead, as pseudoscience—a practice that does not follow the traditional scientific method of research and that therefore cannot be considered real science. Most ghost hunters are considered amateurs or hobbyists. Paranormal investigation, however, is not absent from the academic world. The University of Virginia's School of Medicine has a Division of Perceptual Studies to scientifically research unexplained phenomena such as life after death. Active research projects are under way at the University of Arizona's Department of Psychology to study, among other things, whether spirits survive after death and whether living people can communicate with them. Over the years, Stanford, Duke, Princeton, and Harvard universities and the University of California, Los Angeles, have all had departments to study various aspects of paranormal phenomena, as have respected universities in the United Kingdom, Sweden, the Netherlands, and Australia.

None of these institutions or programs has provided undeniable proof that haunted houses are real. Yet the study of after-death experiences is alive and well among the world's most respected educational and research institutions. Proof of haunted houses may be elusive, but many scientists continue to maintain that hauntings are not impossible. After all, the idea that earth revolves around the sun was once dismissed by the world's leading scientists too, but it turned out to be true.

Armed with sound-recording devices, people are able to obtain evidence of strange noises in houses or buildings they believe could be haunted. Recorders not only capture unexplained sounds such as knocking and thumps but also voices—often voices that are not audible to anyone in the room. Such sounds are known as electronic voice phenomena, or EVPs, and they are one of the main forms of evidence paranormal investigators try to obtain when they study houses that are reportedly haunted. Anyone with a sound-recording device can capture EVPs of everything from laughter or cries for help to conversations between multiple people or even spiritual entities.

Some models of recorders are voice-activated, meaning they begin to record only when they detect a nearby sound. Recording devices left in empty rooms sometimes record what seem to be unexplained voices that share similarities with other voices captured many years ago. "In my opinion, it is highly significant to find . . . a striking parallel between the characteristics of some of those very first voices and voices recorded many years later,"[30] says Anabela Cardoso, who specializes in studying unexplained electronic communications. Many people believe these mysterious recorded sounds to be evidence that hauntings are real.

Visible Evidence of Ghosts

Most houses believed to be haunted are plagued by unexplained noises, but strange visual phenomena are almost as common. People who claim to witness evidence of hauntings often cite spectacles such as shadows that move, shift, and appear or disappear suddenly and unexplainably. They may witness objects that move by themselves, break suddenly, appear to float, or are thrown. Clouds of fog or mist may seem to appear out of nowhere. Many people even see apparitions, lifelike images that seem to be real people until they pass through walls or vanish. Paranormal researchers have long been interested in capturing a visible record of such happenings in an attempt to prove that witnesses are not merely imagining things and that what they claim to see is really there.

In the 1830s the invention of photography made it possible to capture visual evidence of paranormal phenomena. The first cameras were not useful for ghost hunters—it took a very long time for a camera to imprint an image onto film, and most alleged appearances of ghosts are only momentary. Camera technology gradually became more advanced, however, and improvements continued through the 1900s and into the 2000s. Small, portable, and affordable cameras were invented that had a built-in flash for recording images at night or in dim places. With these new cameras, almost anyone could easily capture a precise instant in time with just the click of a button. Capturing unexplainable shadows and ghostly faces or bodies on film before they disappeared became easier than ever.

People also discovered strange images in their developed photographs, showing things that had not been visible to anyone who was present when the photograph was taken. These included unexplainable mist or fog, orbs (glowing circles of light), shadows, and even images of people. Some of these were written off as tricks of light, dust on the camera lens, or effects of the camera's flash. Others were more difficult to explain. "Photographs of ghosts or haunted areas are [rare] because of the great element of chance in obtaining any results at all," said the late Hans Holzer, a paranormal researcher. "But the fact that genuine photographs of what are commonly called ghosts have been taken by a number of people, under conditions excluding fraud or faulty equipment, of course, is food for serious thought."[31]

> "The fact that genuine photographs of what are commonly called ghosts have been taken by a number of people, under conditions excluding fraud or faulty equipment, of course, is food for serious thought."[31]
>
> —Paranormal researcher Hans Holzer.

Over the decades, improved camera technology led to sharper images and better colors. Motion photography was also combined with audio-recording technology to create video cameras, which became very popular devices for the investigation of reportedly haunted places. Voices or sounds could be recorded along with video evidence that showed no living person was in view to make the noises. Video cameras could also record phenomena such as objects moving by themselves. The ability to record moving pictures paired with sound was a big step in gathering evidence of unexplained phenomena. "If ghosts are ever to produce some hard, visual evidence, it will probably come from this medium," says paranormal researcher J. Allan Danelek.[32]

Photography, like audio recording, underwent a major shift to digital technology around the turn of the twenty-first century.

Digital cameras and video cameras take photographs or record video that can be viewed or played back instantly on the devices themselves but can also be enhanced with computer programs to do things like sharpen blurry images or magnify parts of an image. Most modern cell phones are equipped with built-in digital cameras, making it easy for people to capture images of unexplained phenomena anywhere. Paranormal investigators rely on cameras and video cameras to make careful records of their experiences as they explore reportedly haunted places. This technology has made it possible for people to obtain actual evidence of the strange and ghostly things they claim to see in haunted houses. "Without these tools, proving and disproving paranormal occurrences would be difficult to achieve,"[33] says paranormal investigator Stephen Lancaster.

Assessing the Feel of a Haunting

Strange sights and sounds are not the only things people experience in buildings that are claimed to be haunted. Sites of hauntings historically have been blamed for causing physical ailments such as headaches and nausea, as well as a general feeling of fear, uneasiness, or being watched. Some witnesses claim to have felt something touch or push them. People have also long reported that haunted houses—even just a particular room or corner of a room in a haunted house—feel noticeably and unexplainably colder than their surroundings.

Reports of people sensing strange things in certain places, especially if their claims can be paired with audio or video evidence, have led paranormal investigators to develop theories about what might be causing the strange sensations. Many of these theories are based on the scientific principles of energy and magnetism. If ghosts exist, many paranormal investigators believe that they require energy to manifest, or show themselves in some way, such as by making noise, moving an object, or appearing as an image. One theory is that spirits must absorb energy from the people or the space around them to perform any sort of task. Electrical appliances such as lightbulbs or televisions have often been reported to flicker or turn off during or immediately before an unexplained

People who have experienced the presence of a haunted spirit describe strange sensations. These include cold spots in a room, a sense of being watched, and even a touch or light push.

experience in a reportedly haunted house. People who experience or study paranormal activity also claim that batteries in devices such as cell phones, cameras, and flashlights drain very quickly in places that are said to be haunted or when unexplained activity occurs in such a place.

Many believers in the paranormal also claim that a ghostly presence could explain the sudden drop in temperature people claim to feel in haunted places. "The theory is that in order to manifest, the ghost needs energy," says paranormal investigator Debi Chestnut. "The ghost, or other entity, will suck all the energy out of the room like a vacuum, causing the room to become cold; in extreme cases, a room will become so cold that you'll be able to see your breath."[34] Paranormal investigators use a variety of instruments to obtain evidence of phenomena such as temperature changes. Standard ghost-hunting equipment includes digital thermometers, which quickly measure the temperature of the air in a room. In places that are said to be haunted, people have recorded close-up footage of the screen of a digital thermometer as the temperature reading rapidly declines.

Infrared thermometers are even more reliable than digital thermometers at measuring temperature changes. All matter radiates or emits a certain amount of energy, which is measurable as heat. Infrared thermometers are devices that measure the amount of heat an object emits by aiming a beam of infrared light at it. (Infrared light is invisible to human eyes.) The light is reflected back to a sensor on the device, which measures the amount of energy being returned by converting it to a measurement of heat. The user of the device can aim the thermometer at objects (even moving ones) or even at seemingly empty air to determine how much energy, or heat, is being reflected back.

Whereas a digital thermometer measures the overall temperature in a room, an infrared thermometer can measure specific objects that are warmer than their surroundings. Sometimes, an infrared thermometer will measure a warm spot in what seems to be an empty room, indicating some sort of physical item or body that is invisible to human eyes but has measurable heat energy. Infrared thermometers with scanning ability go a step further. The scanner can be placed on a table or other surface, and it sends its beam of light around a room in a continuous circle. If it encounters an object or any unexplained increase in energy and temperature, it will buzz or beep to indicate that it registered something. Sudden, unexplained infrared temperature increases in an otherwise empty room signal to an investigator that something paranormal might be happening.

> "The theory is that in order to manifest, the ghost needs energy. The ghost, or other entity, will suck all the energy out of the room like a vacuum, causing the room to become cold."[34]
>
> —*Paranormal investigator Debi Chestnut.*

Spectral Energy

Another tool many modern paranormal investigators use to measure unexplained phenomena in a building is an EMF meter—a device that measures changes in the electromagnetic field (EMF) of the space. Similar to the way all matter gives off energy in the form of heat, every place on the planet has a measurable magnetic and electric force. The earth itself is a giant magnet, due to the electricity emitted by its metallic inner core. All objects on earth also emit an electromagnetic force of their own. Magnetic and electrical forces exist everywhere and are impossible to escape. When objects move within a space, however, they create subtle changes in the flow of electrical energy in the space. EMF detectors are devices that can measure such changes.

Because EMF forces exist in any space, a paranormal investigator who uses a handheld EMF detector must take careful measurements of the house or room being investigated to establish a baseline—a measurement of the electromagnetic energy that is normal for the particular place. Things like electrical appliances and wiring can affect EMF readings, so one house or even one part of a room within a house can have a unique EMF reading. A high baseline measurement does not indicate a supernatural presence. However, once the EMF baseline has been established, further changes, especially sudden or fleeting ones, could indicate that something is physically moving through the EMF detector's range of measurement. "Electro-magnetic field (EMF) meters are standard fare for all ghost hunters and an invaluable tool in determining when 'something' has entered the room so cameras can be pointed and tape recorders turned on,"[35] says Danelek.

Low-Tech Methods

Devices like high-quality digital cameras and voice recorders, infrared thermometers, and EMF detectors can cost hundreds to thousands of dollars, but not all ghost hunters believe these high-tech devices are necessary to detect the presence of a spirit in a building rumored to be haunted. Some paranormal investigators say that a simple compass can show changes in electrical fields as well as any electronic EMF detector. If the compass needle begins to spin or momentarily changes direction, it indicates a change in the magnetic field. This might indicate—perhaps as well as an electronic EMF detector can—the presence of a spirit that has its own electrical energy.

Other people believe that the general feelings of uneasiness, discomfort, or fear some people claim to feel in reportedly haunted places are based on instincts. People have active imaginations and could be vulnerable to having strange feelings in peculiar places they already believe might be haunted. Animals, on the other hand, are not believed to have imaginations, yet they often react strangely in places that people also claim make them uneasy. "Usually, dogs and cats respond to spirits in a negative way," say paranormal investigators Jason Hawes, Grant Wilson, and Michael Jan Friedman, known for their roles on the television show *Ghost Hunters*. "It's difficult to say why. Maybe they're sensitive to the paranormal in ways human beings aren't."[36]

Household pets, particularly dogs and cats, have been known to respond physically to unseen things in locations people claim are haunted. Pets may act frightened or aggressive for no obvious reason. Dogs may whine, bark, growl, bare their teeth, and raise the hair on the back of their neck as if they are facing a threat, even if nothing is visible to the people in the room. Cats, similarly, may

Dogs and other pets often respond to occurrences that people do not see or hear. Dogs might growl, whine, bark, or bare their teeth if they sense a presence.

Pets as Ghost Detectives

People who are convinced they have encountered a haunting often use the strange behavior of household pets as a clue that a ghost or spirit could be present. Animal experts, however, say that peculiar pet behavior could have many explanations that have nothing to do with ghosts. Pets' senses, especially smell and hearing, are many times more powerful than those of people. It is plausible that when animals seem focused on things the people around them cannot sense, they are tuned in to perfectly natural sounds, smells, or even vibrations coming from far away.

Not everyone agrees that strange pet behavior can be so easily explained. For one thing, most animals are curious. The ability to detect a sound or smell that people cannot sense would seem to incite pets to explore, not to cower in fear, back away, or refuse to enter a particular room. Also, not all animals react in fear to what seem like invisible presences. They sometimes behave affectionately and even appear to be interacting or playing with a person no one can see.

Importantly, animals lack humans' reasoning ability. Whereas a person might ignore a strange experience, believing it to be all in his or her head, pets respond physically and immediately to what they sense. Whether animals perceive ghosts better than people—or whether they are simply better at sensing things with natural, explainable causes—remains, like many other paranormal matters, a subject of debate.

growl and hiss while their hair stands on end, or may run away suddenly as if startled. Both dogs and cats may avoid certain areas of a house, such as refusing to go upstairs or cross the threshold into a certain room. Many people believe that such unexplainable behavior, especially by pets that are otherwise calm and friendly, indicates that hard-to-measure strange or ominous feelings in certain places are not just a figment of someone's imagination.

Accumulated Evidence

People who investigate supposedly haunted sites use a wide variety of modern technological devices as a way to collect hard scientific data about spiritual infestations. A single strange or peculiar finding may not indicate a ghostly presence within a building. However, many people consider a combination of phenomena, including recorded voices and images, temperature changes, shifting EMF readings, and unexplained behavior of animals, to be compelling. Twenty-first century technology has made it easier than ever to show that measurable phenomena do take place without a clear explanation in many houses or other buildings people claim are haunted.

Chapter 4

Are There Other Explanations?

"Hauntings do not require genuine ghosts, underground streams, low frequency sound waves, or weak magnetic fields. Instead, all it takes is the power of suggestion."

—Psychology professor Richard Wiseman.

Richard Wiseman, "The Haunted Brain," *Skeptical Inquirer*, September/October 2011. www.csicop.org.

"People who devote their lives to the occult pray that some-day a case will come along that is so clear-cut, even the greatest doubter will have to believe."

—Paranormal investigator Ed Warren.

Ed Warren, Lorraine Warren, and Robert David Chase, *Ghost Hunters: True Stories from the World's Most Famous Demonologists*. E-book edition. Los Angeles, CA: Graymalkin Media, 2014.

Most people who believe in haunted houses have experienced unexplained phenomena themselves or are inclined to believe that at least some anecdotal evidence—the many stories told about haunted experiences—must be real. No matter how often or reliably the same story might be repeated, however, anecdotal evidence is very different than *scientific* evidence, or information gathered from conducting experiments. In science, experiments must meet many criteria in order for other scientists to consider them good experiments whose results can be trusted. This is something paranormal investigation often fails to do.

Scientific Experimentation

The first principle of a scientific experiment is that it must be repeated exactly the same way many times, and the results of the experiment (the data) must be recorded. Second, the method for conducting the experiment must be precisely described so that other scientists can try the same process to see whether they get the same results. Good experiments rely on taking careful measurements using accurate tools or devices that have been proven to be reliable. Scientific experiments also require a single variable (the thing that can change or that is being tested) while all other conditions are being controlled. This way, if a change or a phenomenon happens, the scientist will not puzzle over the actual cause of it.

Perhaps most importantly, scientific experiments also must be impartial, meaning that the researchers must not have decided before the experiment whether the thing they are seeking to test is true or untrue. Emotions must not sway their testing methods or results. The study of hauntings, however, is almost always tinged with emotion and is rarely impartial. Believers might wish very strongly to prove once and for all that ghosts exist and nonbelievers may desperately want to prove the opposite, to the point that researchers on both sides of the debate might alter evidence (either on purpose or without realizing it) to show that they are right. Furthermore, being in a place with a reputation of being haunted, even if one does not believe in ghosts, could make a researcher feel uneasy, which could affect the reliability of any results he or she obtains. "When you're in a place that has a little notoriety to it, you might get a little jumpy,"[37] says Ken DeCosta, founder of an investigative organization called RISEUP Paranormal in Rhode Island. Fear or nervousness, skeptics say, could lead researchers to conclusions based more on emotion than fact.

> "When you're in a place that has a little notoriety to it, you might get a little jumpy."[37]
>
> —*Paranormal researcher Ken DeCosta.*

Paranormal investigators who use technological instruments to record strange phenomena in haunted houses have come closer than ever to showing that strange and unexplained events occur in places that are said to be haunted. In fact, many skeptics agree that these investigators have been successful at capturing evidence of something that cannot be easily explained. However, skeptics do not readily conclude that ghosts are a suitable explanation for these phenomena. If ghosts exist, people have not yet discovered precise characteristics that can be measured or studied repeatedly and consistently, no matter how high-tech the measuring devices may be. The manner in which ghosts are said to make their presence known varies widely from place to place and from ghost to ghost. Their appearance is therefore very difficult or even impossible to predict and to measure exactly the same way numerous times.

For these reasons, the phenomenon of haunted houses has long been considered impossible to test scientifically. In the absence of hard scientific evidence, a majority of people continue to believe that there are multiple possible explanations for strange phenomena other than that a house is haunted.

Shedding Light on the Mystery

One of the main reasons many people are skeptical about the evidence collected within haunted houses is that paranormal investigators conduct many if not most of their experiments in the dark. Many people who study haunted houses say this is because most unexplained phenomena in haunted houses tend to happen at night when the lights are turned off. Skeptics, however, point out that it is very easy in the dark to confuse something that is perfectly normal with something that could be sinister or ghostly. For example, the sudden appearance of a moving shadow could be a ghost, but it could also be caused by the headlights of a car driving on a road in the distance. Shapes of everyday things like clothes or furniture can also seem mysterious in the dark but are easily explained once the lights are turned on.

Another criticism of studying haunted houses only at night is that dark conditions tend to make people feel nervous and highly attentive to all of their senses. If they hear, see, or feel things they perceive to be unusual, they might jump to the conclusion that they are in the presence of ghosts. "Reports of frightening ex-

Most reports of house hauntings involve attics, basements, crawl spaces, and closets. These spaces are usually small, tight, and dark—features that might spark fear and imagined occurrences.

periences taking place in a home are also mostly based around confining and dark locations such as attics, basements/crawl spaces, and closets," says paranormal investigator John E.L. Tenney. "This can be attributed to our own human psychological fear of dark and constrictive spaces."[38] It is possible that the same phenomena that frighten someone in the dark might not capture a person's attention the same way if experienced in an open, well-lit space.

Most scientific researchers see no logical reason why ghosts, if they do exist, would not also haunt places during the daytime. Therefore, many people are suspicious as to why there is limited film footage of ghostly experiences occurring in well-lit conditions where visibility is at its best. "There are no other objects or entities in the world that anyone would think are better observed in darkness instead of light; why would ghosts be any different?" asks Benjamin Radford, a scientific paranormal investigator and editor of *Skeptical Inquirer* magazine. "Searching at night in the dark puts investigators at an immediate and obvious disadvantage in trying to identify and understand what's going on around them."[39]

Characteristics of Old Houses

Another main criticism of the evidence of haunted houses is the typical age and physical condition of the buildings themselves. Some brand-new houses or buildings develop a reputation for being haunted, but most buildings widely considered to harbor ghosts are old structures. Believers in ghosts often say this is because older buildings have a history. If many people have lived in a place, and especially if someone has died within the home, one or more spirits may feel attached to the building and want to linger there once their physical body has died.

"There are no other objects or entities in the world that anyone would think are better observed in darkness instead of light; why would ghosts be any different?"[39]

— *Scientific paranormal investigator Benjamin Radford.*

Skeptics believe the very fact that most haunted houses are older homes could explain many if not all of the peculiar phenomena that occur within them, starting with sounds. "Houses are made up of a combination of wood, glass, concrete and other materials that contract and expand throughout the day, all at different rates," says home improvement expert Shannon Lee. "This leads to creaking, popping, and other strange sounds that might surprise you when you least expect it."[40] Most older houses are not airtight, either, so

The Sound of a Haunting

Certain houses or buildings have a long history of making people feel uneasy. Residents or visitors describe feeling chills, sorrow, shakiness, and an overwhelming sense of fear or dread. Such experiences are often blamed on the presence of spirits attempting to drive away the living. Scientists, however, have another theory about what could be causing people's discomfort: infrasound.

Infrasound is a level of sound that occurs on a wavelength too low for the human ear to perceive it. Many natural phenomena, from storms to geological movement that happens deep underground, can create infrasound. Scientists have also discovered how to generate infrasound and have studied its effects on people. When exposed to infrasound, people often claim they experience chills, sorrow, shakiness, and a sense of fear or dread—much as people might claim to feel in places rumored to be haunted. Scientists say it is possible that a natural source of infrasound exists near certain reportedly haunted sites and that this, not ghosts, is the cause of physical distress.

even a slight breeze outdoors could cause air to move through small cracks and openings, causing peculiar whistling, rustling, or groaning.

Also, because they are not airtight, old houses tend to be drafty. Moving air could explain phenomena such as the sensation of something brushing against one's skin or clothing and objects moving unexplainably, as well as shifts in temperature or rooms that seem noticeably colder than neighboring areas. "The most common culprits are cracked and drafty window frames, poor quality windows, uninsulated electrical outlets and gaps around doors," says home improvement and real estate columnist Adam Verwymeren. "To track down leaks in your home," he recommends, "grab an infrared thermometer and hunt for cold spots to see what needs to be fixed."[41] Ironically, many paranormal investigators say the cold spots found with such thermometers can be signs of ghosts, but the real explanation could be walls letting in cold air.

Older houses also are more likely than new houses to have run-down heating, plumbing, and electrical systems. Aging water pipes and air ducts can thump or rattle within walls, leading to a variety of strange sounds that could be confused with footsteps or even the sound of human voices. Old electrical wiring

Doors that seemingly open and close on their own might have a simple explanation—other than haunted spirits. As buildings age and settle, small changes that occur in walls, ceilings, and floors might lead to doors that swing more freely on their hinges.

and faulty circuits in older homes could also contribute to seemingly unexplained phenomena, including flickering lights and appliances that suddenly shut down. All of these are often believed to be signs of ghostly activity in haunted houses, but they may have more to do with characteristics of aging and deteriorating buildings than with the activity of spirits.

Another feature of older homes is that the ground beneath them, as well as structural pieces of the buildings themselves, can settle or shift with time. When most houses are constructed, the builders ensure that the floors and ceilings are level—flat and even with no slope from one end to the other—and that the walls are square, that is, their corners form right angles where they meet the ceiling and the floor. As buildings age and settle, however, small shifts in walls, ceilings, and floors can result in surfaces that slant and corners that are not square. Even changes too minor for most people to notice can lead to doors that swing open or closed because they are not plumb. Furthermore, doors can be difficult to latch completely when door frames are no longer perfectly square, so a door that a homeowner believes was shut could swing back open by itself. A settling house might also explain phenomena such as round objects that roll across floors or off of countertops for no obvious reason. Such events are sometimes attributed to ghosts when in fact gravity is to blame, especially in houses that have stood for many years.

Electromagnetic Fields

Skeptics say that even the seemingly science-based evidence collected with devices that measure electric or magnetic fields and infrared temperature changes can have other explanations. For example, EMF readers detect changes in electromagnetic radiation that many ghost hunters claim could indicate an unseen presence. However, skeptics point out that most things give off a certain level of radiation at different frequencies (the rates at which sound waves, radio waves, or light waves repeat as they move through a material or space). All electrical appliances and devices, power lines, radio waves, wireless networks, fluorescent lights, faulty power switches, cell phones, and even the investigators' own cameras and other equipment emit EMF radiation. For that matter, living things and even the earth itself can cause changes that are detectable with an EMF reader—it simply must be tuned to register that specific frequency.

EMF readers might indeed detect a sudden change in electromagnetic radiation, skeptics say, but the cause could be countless things other than a restless spirit. "There is (at least to the best of my knowledge) no theory on how, and if, electromagnetic fields would vary at the point of a paranormal event occurring," says John Fraser, a paranormal investigator and council member of the Society for Psychical Research. "In fact there is a working hypothesis that electromagnetic fields, when present for nonparanormal reasons, trigger effects on the brain that could make it more susceptible to interpreting a natural event as a paranormal one. . . . Its [the EMF reader's] function, ironically, is as a potential ghost debunker rather than the ghost detector so many had thought it to be."[42]

Photographic and Video Evidence

Cameras (still and video) and sound recorders are also frequently used in efforts to document hauntings. Photographs or video footage sometimes show misty clouds, orbs, streaks of light, shadows, human faces in mirrors and windows, and other oddities. Photographers often say these images were not visible to them when they took the picture, and they cite such appearances as persuasive visual evidence of ghosts.

Photographic, audio, and video evidence of hauntings does seem to offer some of the strongest proof that can be gathered, but this type of evidence also has its critics. Skeptics say it is far more likely that these anomalies are caused by camera technology or dust or water droplets on the lens. A camera flash reflects off of these particles and amplifies them into what appear to be circles of light in the picture. "Naturalistic orbs are generally the result of using digital cameras with a built-in flash," explains David Rountree, founder of Scientific Paranormal Investigative Research Information and Technology (S.P.I.R.I.T.). "The increase in orb photos may be directly related to the common availability of digital cameras and associated rise in the number of pictures taken," he says. "It is estimated that fully one-third of those contain anomalies that are orb like in appearance. . . . As far as I know, there is no evidence to directly link an orb to a dead person."[43]

Another phenomenon—unexplained mist or fog that appears in a photograph—could be caused by condensation of breath, either of the photographer or of other people nearby. The streaks of light that sometimes appear in photographs could be caused by an object moving through the camera's field at the time the photograph is taken. A flying insect, a moving car, or even the glare from a bracelet or watch can unknowingly be captured in a photo or in video footage. When photographs are taken at night or in dim conditions, as they often are in connection with suspected hauntings, the mysterious image might be nothing more than a reflection resulting from the flash rather than a ghost.

> "As far as I know, there is no evidence to directly link an orb to a dead person."[43]
>
> —David Rountree, founder of Scientific Paranormal Investigative Research Information and Technology.

Unexplained faces that appear in photographs of mirrors or windows could also be caused by reflections. Any series of mirrors or reflective surfaces like glass doors and windows, when angled in particular ways, can cast reflected images from one part of a room to another. An unexpected person seen in a mirror might actually have been standing around the corner at the time the photograph was taken, and his or her image was cast from one reflective surface to another—a strange but explainable phenomenon.

Similarly, photographs taken from outside an abandoned house that seem to capture the image of a person or a face in a window might have explanations other than a spectral entity peering through it. Other possibilities include shadows, reflections, or tricks of light against the reflective glass. Such tricks of light can be convincing. In the 1860s producers of plays in London baffled audiences when they learned how to create the illusion of ghosts

Psychic Connections

A common and often criticized component of haunted house exploration is the presence of people who claim to have psychic abilities. These abilities might include a knack for sensing, seeing, and even talking to ghosts that might dwell in a building. Many such people have been debunked as frauds over the years. But because psychics claim to experience things other people cannot, it is difficult to prove or disprove that they have special powers.

Despite the uncertainty surrounding psychics, they are prominent on television shows about ghost hunting, and at least some of what they say can seem plausible. For instance, a psychic might claim to communicate with the spirit of a troubled girl. A later study of the home's history may reveal that a girl died there. When such incidents are shown on television, it is easy to conclude that the psychic must indeed have communicated with spirits. However, psychics might make many incorrect statements before alighting on one that seems true, and viewers hardly ever see those guesses because they are edited out of the final footage. It is also possible that psychic investigators study a home's history before touring it, thus giving them insight into compelling stories of the kinds of spirits that might dwell there.

Psychic knowledge of ghosts in a haunted house is difficult to prove and easy to criticize. Nevertheless, the recurring appearance of psychics on TV shows about haunted places suggests that many viewers readily accept psychics' self-proclaimed ability to communicate with ghosts no one else can see or hear.

on stage. They accomplished this feat by using glass angled to reflect the image of an actor out of the viewers' line of sight. "The reflections appeared as detached images floating on air. A product of the science of optics (angles of reflection, the transparency of glass),"[44] says art history and cinema professor Tom Gunning. It is possible the same scientific properties could also explain ghostly apparitions captured in photographs of windows and mirrors taken in reportedly haunted buildings.

Video cameras are as susceptible as still-photograph cameras to effects of light, shadow, and reflection, especially because most film footage that captures seemingly ghostly images or phenomena is recorded at night or in dim rooms. Modern video cameras have various settings for filming in different types of conditions. In the hands of an inexperienced user, however, the video camera can easily be adjusted to the wrong settings. This, or even faulty technology, can result in any number of strange on-screen images that have nothing to do with the paranormal world. Some photographs and video footage do contain images that even skeptics find difficult to explain. For these instances, however, skeptics also say that there are countless possible theories as to what caused the strange imagery. It therefore makes little sense to leap to the conclusion that the only explanation is ghosts.

Tricky Sounds

For many people the sound of strange voices captured on audio recording devices is even more compelling evidence of a haunting than is visual imagery from a camera. Electronic voice phenomena, or EVPs, are frequently obtained in places that are said to be haunted. Recorded sounds have included what seem to be whispers, shouts, screams, crying babies, laughing children, and even partial conversations. These voices are sometimes recorded in rooms or buildings that seem to be empty or in the presence of investigators who are not speaking at the time. Skeptics say that even these seeming phenomena could have explanations, however. A sensitive recorder might be able to capture noises from another room or even from outside the building, though these voices seem to come from within the room itself.

It is also possible that unexplained sounds seeming to be voices, whispers, whimpers, or cries actually might not be human voices at all. Rather they might result from rustling, buzzing, or other noises from some undetermined but explicable source. Many examples of EVPs captured in buildings rumored to be haunted are identified as voices but are interpreted differently by different people. Often they must be clarified by computer programs in order to sound intelligible. "In an attempt to make these messages more audible, they are enhanced and amplified using audio software programs," says linguist Karen Stollznow. "This can inadvertently, or purposefully, manipulate the recordings to make the results more persuasive."[45]

Popular television shows about haunted house investigations typically allow viewers to listen to EVPs captured at a site, but they translate what they believe the supposed voice actually says. Some listeners, if asked about the same sound without being told what to expect, might come to a different conclusion altogether, even claiming that they hear only static and no human voice at all. "It's not that the messages are inaudible or garbled to begin with, it's that they aren't messages," Stollznow says. "The causes of these recordings are natural, not supernatural."[46]

> "It's not that the messages are inaudible or garbled to begin with, it's that they aren't messages."[46]
>
> —Linguist Karen Stollznow.

The Power of Suggestion

The fact that millions of viewers experience haunted houses mainly by watching televised programs about them points to one of the largest criticisms skeptics have concerning contemporary claims of hauntings. They believe that these types of shows rely on sensationalism or the use of stories or details that may be false or exaggerated to make the events more interesting and attract more viewers. Especially when explorations of haunted sites are televised, the film is edited to make things look or sound especially shocking or frightening, and eerie music adds to the suspense. Shows about hauntings attract millions of viewers, and the more people watch such programs, the more they come to believe that assumptions about ghosts and haunted buildings are actual facts.

The many television shows and movies about haunted houses and ghostly spirits might actually encourage people to believe in these phenomena. Televised ghost-hunting shows, in particular, might influence what viewers believe about hauntings.

The truth, skeptics say, is that there are no known facts about ghosts. As yet haunted houses have never been defined as having consistent, measurable properties, behaviors, and characteristics. Most skeptics believe haunted houses are the product of human imagination, superstition, and lore passed down over many centuries. These age-old legends in many cases seem to be upheld by modern technology, but skeptics say most of the evidence collected by modern devices falls far short of true science. Tales of hauntings, they say, are really just that—tales. But in the absence of definitive proof either way, no one knows for certain.

The Search Goes On

Despite facing considerable doubts ranging from polite disbelief to outright scoffing, people who believe in haunted houses stay true to their convictions that something unexplainable is out there. Believers are often accused of being gullible, but they in turn say skeptics may rush to find explanations for what seems to be a haunting without fully considering all the evidence. Many believers in haunted houses have personally experienced things they think could only have had a supernatural cause, and no amount of scientific theory can change their minds.

The quest to prove or disprove that hauntings are caused by spirits of the dead may be as old as humanity itself. Unlike many beliefs, myths, and folktales of earlier times that have been debunked by scientific discoveries, stories of haunted houses persist, and they continually defy any complete scientific explanation. The infatuation with haunted places is ongoing, and so is the use of modern technology to explore and attempt to validate the belief in them.

In many places around the world, acceptance of the possibility of haunted houses is still strong enough to make local people shun them, but in the United States and much of Europe, places with a haunted reputation attract tourists by the thousands. Believers and skeptics alike hope to experience ghostly behavior for themselves, answering a timeless question once and for all—do haunted houses exist? Indisputable proof one way or the other may never be found, but believers today join those through the centuries who have insisted that inexplicable things take place in houses alleged to be haunted.

Source Notes

Introduction: What Are Haunted Houses?

1. *Merriam-Webster's Collegiate Dictionary*, 11th ed. Springfield, MA: Merriam-Webster, Inc., 2003, p. 571.

2. Gary D. Joiner and Cheryl H. White, *Historic Haunts of Shreveport*. Charleston, SC: Haunted America, 2010, p. 17.

3. *Rhode Island Real Estate Basics*. LaCrosse, WI: Dearborn Real Estate, 2002, p. 50.

Chapter One: Why Do People Believe in Haunted Houses?

4. Robert James Wlodarski and Anne Powell Wlodarski, *Dinner and Spirits: A Guide to America's Most Haunted Restaurants, Taverns, and Inns*. Lincoln, NE: iUniverse, 2001, p. x.

5. A.R. George, *The Babylonian Gilgamesh Epic: Introduction, Critical Edition and Cuneiform Texts, Volume II*. Oxford, UK: Oxford University Press, 2003, p. 776.

6. Robert M. Schoch and Robert Aquinas McNally, *Pyramid Quest: Secrets of the Great Pyramid and the Dawn of Civilization*. Kindle edition. New York: Penguin, 2005.

7. Samuel Butler, trans., *Homer's Odyssey*. Easyread Comfort Edition. Surry Hills, Australia: Accessible Publishing Systems, 2008, p. 227.

8. The Younger Pliny, *The Letters of the Younger Pliny*, trans. Betty Radice. E-book edition. New York: Penguin Putnam, 1969.

9. Joshua J. Mark, "Ghosts in the Ancient World," *Ancient History Encyclopedia*, October 30, 2014. www.ancient.eu.

10. Quoted in Franc Johnson Newcomb, *Navajo Omens and Taboos*. Santa Fe, NM: Rydal, 1940, p. 49.

11. Mu-Chou Poo, Introduction, in *Rethinking Ghosts in World Religions*, ed. Mu-Chou Poo. Leiden, Netherlands: Koninklijke Brill NV, 2009, p. 6.

12. Charles A. Coulombe, *Haunted Castles of the World: Ghostly Legends and Phenomena from Keeps and Fortresses around the Globe*. Guilford, CT: The Lyons Press, 2004, p. 4.

13. Larry Dreller, *Secrets of a Medium*. York Beach, ME: Red Wheel/Weiser, 2003, p. 24.

14. Sofie Lachapelle, *Investigating the Supernatural: From Spiritism and Occultism to Psychical Research and Metaphysics in France, 1853–1931*. Baltimore, MD: Johns Hopkins University Press, 2011, pp. 86–87.

Chapter Two: Encounters with Haunted Houses

15. Greg Jenkins, *Florida's Ghostly Legends and Haunted Folklore: South and Central Florida*. Sarasota, FL: Pineapple Press, 2005, p. 154.

16. Loyd Auerbach, *Ghost Hunting: How to Investigate the Paranormal*. Oakland, CA: Ronin Publishing, 2004, p. 33.

17. Leo Ruickbie, "Britain's Spookiest Places," *The Daily Express*, August 23, 2013. www.express.co.uk.

18. Keith Grossl, *The Final Hours of Darkness*. Bloomington, IN: AuthorHouse, 2014, p. 82.

19. Quoted in "Amityville Horror: Horror or Hoax?," *ABC News*, October 31, 2014. http://abcnews.go.com.

20. Victoria Cosner Love and Lorelei Shannon, *Mad Madame Lalaurie: New Orleans' Most Famous Murderess Revealed*. Charleston, SC: The History Press, 2011, p. 106.

21. William J. Birnes and Joel Martin, *The Haunting of Twentieth-Century America*. E-book edition. New York: Forge, 2011.

22. Mary Jo Ignoffo, *Captive of the Labyrinth: Sarah L. Winchester, Heiress to the Rifle Fortune*. Columbia, MO: University of Missouri Press, 2010, p. xiii.

23. Deonna Kelli Sayed, *So You Want to Hunt Ghosts?* E-book edition. Woodbury, MN: Llewellyn Publications, 2012.

24. Ed Pearce, "Haunted Nevada: A Skeptic Spends Dark Hours in a Haunted House," *KOLO 8 News Now*, November 2, 2014. www.kolotv.com.

25. Pearce, "Haunted Nevada."

26. Quoted in Paul Kimball and Dale Stevens, directors, "Death Farm," episode 5 of *Ghost Cases*. Halifax, Nova Scotia: Eastlink TV, 2010.

Chapter Three: The Study of Haunted Houses

27. Joel Martin and William J. Birnes, *The Haunting of Twenty-First-Century America*. New York: Forge, 2013, pp. 73–74.

28. Philip Ball, *Invisible: The Dangerous Allure of the Unseen*. Chicago, IL: University of Chicago Press, 2013, p. 86.

29. Mark Rosney, Rob Bethell, and Jebby Robinson, *A Beginner's Guide to Paranormal Investigation*. E-book edition. Gloucestershire, UK: Amberley Publishing, 2012.

30. Anabela Cardoso, *Electronic Voices: Contact with Another Dimension?* Hants, UK: O-Books, 2010, p. 31.

31. Hans Holzer, *Ghosts: True Encounters with the World Beyond*. E-book edition. New York: Black Dog & Leventhal Publishers, 2004.

32. J. Allan Danelek, *The Case for Ghosts: An Objective Look at the Paranormal*. Woodbury, MN: Llewellyn Publications, 2006, p. 114.

33. Stephen Lancaster, *True Casefiles of a Paranormal Investigator*. Woodbury, MN: Llewellyn Publications, 2012, p. 3.

34. Debi Chestnut*, How to Clear Your Home of Ghosts & Spirits: Tips & Techniques from a Professional Ghost Hunter*. E-book edition. Woodbury, MN: Llewellyn Publications, 2014.

35. Danelek, *Case for Ghosts*, p. 118.

36. Jason Hawes, Grant Wilson, and Michael Jan Friedman, *Ghost Files: The Collected Cases from Ghost Hunting and Seeking Spirits*. New York: Gallery Books, 2007, p. 50.

Chapter Four: Are There Other Explanations?

37. Quoted in "Ghost Hunters Don't Jump to Paranormal Conclusion," *Warwick Beacon*, October 26, 2010. http://warwick online.com.

38. Quoted in Carly Ledbetter, "Haunted House Myths Confirmed and Debunked," *The Huffington Post*, October 14, 2014. www.huffingtonpost.com.

39. Benjamin Radford, "Ghost-Hunting Mistakes: Science and Pseudoscience in Ghost Investigations," *Skeptical Inquirer*, November/December 2010. www.csicop.org.

40. Shannon Lee, "5 Strange House Sounds Explained," *Improvement Center*, April 28, 2014. www.improvementcenter.com.

41. Adam Verwymeren, "Most Common Problems in Older Homes," *Fox News*, February 27, 2014. www.foxnews.com.

42. John Fraser, *Ghost Hunting: A Survivor's Guide*. E-book edition. Gloucestershire, UK: The History Press, 2013.

43. David M. Rountree, *Paranormal Technology: Understanding the Science of Ghost Hunting*. Bloomington, IN: iUniverse, 2010, pp. 228–229.

44. Tom Gunning, "To Scan a Ghost: The Ontology of Mediated Vision," in *The Spectralities Reader: Ghosts and Haunting in Contemporary Cultural Theory*, ed. María del Pilar Blanco and Esther Peeren. New York: Bloomsbury, 2013, p. 228.

45. Karen Stollznow, *Language Myths, Mysteries and Magic*. New York: Pallgrave Macmillan, 2014, p. 124.

46. Stollznow, *Language Myths*, p. 124.

For Further Research

Books

Theresa Argie and Eric Olsen, *America's Most Haunted: The Secrets of Famous Paranormal Places*. New York: Berkeley Publishing Group, 2014.

Jeff Belanger, *Encyclopedia of Haunted Places: Ghostly Locales from Around the World*. Franklin Lakes, NJ: Career Press, 2009.

Marley Gibson, Patrick Burns, and Dave Schrader, *The Other Side: A Teen's Guide to Ghost Hunting and the Paranormal*. New York: Graphia, 2009.

Kelly Milner Halls, *Ghostly Evidence: Exploring the Paranormal*. Minneapolis, MN: Millbrook Press, 2014.

Joe Nickell, *The Science of Ghosts: Searching for Spirits of the Dead*. New York: Prometheus Books, 2012.

DVDs

The History Channel, director, *History Classics: America's Most Haunted Places*. New York: A&E Home Entertainment, 2011.

Haunted Houses. New York: A&E Home Video, 2008.

Internet Sources

Melissa Locker, "The Boo-tiful Business of Ghost Tourism," *Fortune*, October 31, 2014. http://fortune.com/2014/10/31/the -boo-tiful-business-of-ghost-tourism/.

Benjamin Radford, "Are Ghosts Real? Science Says No-o-o-o," *Live Science*, October 21, 2014. www.livescience.com/26697 -are-ghosts-real.html.

"Top 10 Haunted Places," *Time*. http://content.time.com/time /specials/packages/0,28757,1855221,00.html.

Websites

American Society for Psychical Research. http://www.aspr .com/. Founded in 1885, this is the oldest research organization in the United States for exploring extraordinary or as yet unexplained phenomena known as psychic or paranormal.

Committee for Skeptical Inquiry. www.csicop.org/. This organization's mission is to use science, reason, and critical investigation to examine controversial and extraordinary claims about paranormal phenomena like hauntings.

Index

Picture Credits

About the Author

Jenny MacKay has written more than thirty books for teens and preteens on topics ranging from crime scene investigation and technological marvels to historical issues and the science of sports. She lives in Sparks, Nevada.